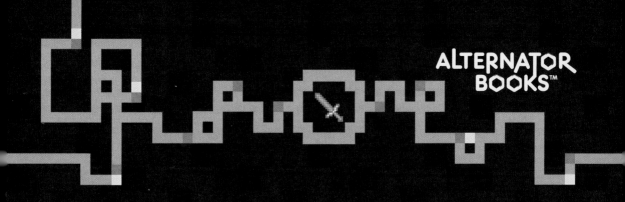

ALTERNATOR
BOOKS™

THE UNOFFICIAL GUIDE TO MINECRAFT SURVIVAL

LINDA ZAJAC

Lerner Publications ◆ Minneapolis

TO WALT, WHO IS OFTEN AT THE CRAFTING TABLE. THANKS FOR FUELING THE FURNACE, HARVESTING THE WHEAT, AND ENCHANTING MY LIFE.

Lerner Publications Company
A division of Lerner Publishing Group, Inc.
241 First Avenue North
Minneapolis, MN 55401 USA

For reading levels and more information, look up this title at www.lernerbooks.com.

Main body text set in Aptifer Slab LT Pro 11.5/18.
Typeface provided by Linotype AG.

Library of Congress Cataloging-in-Publication Data

Names: Zajac, Linda, 1960– author.
Title: The unofficial guide to Minecraft survival / Linda Zajac.
Description: Minneapolis : Lerner Publications, 2019. | Series: My Minecraft (Alternator Books) | Includes bibliographical references and index. | Audience: Age 7–11. | Audience: Grade 4 to 6.
Identifiers: LCCN 2018022642 (print) | LCCN 2018023488 (ebook) | ISBN 9781541543546 (eb pdf) | ISBN 9781541538870 (lb : alk. paper) | ISBN 9781541546134 (pb : alk. paper)
Subjects: LCSH: Minecraft (Game)—Juvenile literature.
Classification: LCC GV1469.35.M535 (ebook) | LCC GV1469.35.M535 Z354 2019 (print) | DDC 794.8—dc23

LC record available at https://lccn.loc.gov/2018022642

Manufactured in the United States of America
4-48816-35897-11/14/2019

CONTENTS

BEWARE THE NIGHT

INSIDE THE WORLD OF *MINECRAFT*, GRASS AND TREES SURROUND YOU.

Some rocks and coal are nearby. The sun is high in the sky, but you know it won't stay there long. Soon it will get dark. That's when the dangerous creatures come out.

Trees are common objects in *Minecraft*, and it's easy to collect wood from them.

You quickly gather wood from the trees and put together a sword and a pickax. Next, you need to make a shelter. You look around. No cave is nearby, and you aren't sure you have enough wood or time to build a cabin. Instead, you grab your pickax and start digging. You decide to hide underground. Time is running out. If you don't prepare for the night, you might not survive.

CHAPTER 1
TIMBER!

MINECRAFT **IS AN INCREDIBLY POPULAR GAME.** About seventy-four million people play every month. In this world made up of blocks, you have the freedom to create and explore.

In Creative mode, gamers can focus on building and exploring without worrying about their character dying.

There are a few different ways to play. One is Creative mode, where you can stack and arrange blocks any way you want. You have unlimited supplies, and you don't have to worry about monsters. But in Survival mode, you have to gather your own materials, build a shelter, stay healthy, find food, and battle monsters.

The game starts when you land in a brand-new world. This is called **spawning**. It's tempting to run around to explore. Each new game features a unique landscape, so no two games are the same. There may be different arrangements of mountains, islands, and oceans. But exploring in Survival mode can be dangerous! You have only ten minutes of daylight. Once the sun slips below

Minecraft worlds are fun to explore, but your first priority in Survival mode is to stay alive.

Zombies may attack in groups, but they're slow moving and easy to avoid.

the horizon, **hostile mobs**, or monsters such as zombies, skeletons, and creepers, will emerge from the shadows to hunt you down.

To survive your first night, you need to plan and act quickly. You must gather materials so you can build tools and shelter to protect yourself. Wood is one of the most important materials. It helps you make all the other items you need right away. And it is usually easy to find and collect at the beginning of the game. You just need to find a nearby tree.

You don't need any special tools to collect wood. Instead, once you're close, you punch the trunk with your fist until it smashes into blocks. For your first night, all you need is enough wood for a crafting table and some simple tools and weapons.

You can chop wood without a tool, but it goes faster if you have an ax.

STEMCRAFT

Materials in *Minecraft* are similar to materials in the real world. People make homes and tools out of wood, stone, or metal. Some of these materials are stronger, more expensive, or rarer than others.

In *Minecraft*, wood is easy to find and mine. It's not the strongest material, but an **ore** such as diamond ore is much harder to mine. That's why wood is one of the first materials players look for in Survival mode.

Players need diamonds to make the game's strongest tools, but diamonds lie deep underground and are difficult to find.

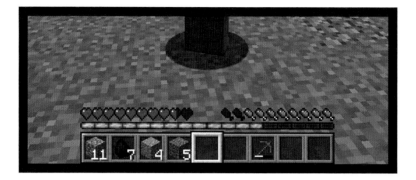

The hotbar has nine boxes for items.

As you gather wood, it will appear in the **hotbar** at the bottom of your screen. These boxes are like pockets in your clothes. You keep the most useful items from your **inventory**, such as tools, food, and weapons, in the hotbar.

CHAPTER 2

CRAFT AND BUILD

ONCE YOU HAVE MATERIALS IN YOUR INVENTORY, YOU CAN BEGIN CRAFTING ITEMS. First, you'll use wood to make a crafting table. The table will allow you to create all the tools you will need throughout the game.

The first basic tools you need in *Minecraft* are a sword to defend yourself against mobs, a pickax for mining stone, and a shovel for digging. You can make all of these tools with wood at first. However, wooden tools soon wear down. You will need to replace or upgrade your tools as you mine stone and other ores.

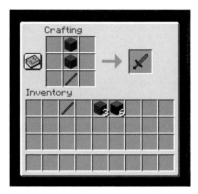

It's easy to make a wooden sword.

A crafting table looks like a wooden block.

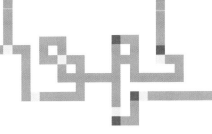

Next, you need a shelter so you can spend the night hidden away from mobs. If you're attacked or become injured and die, you'll respawn in the same place where you started the game. This is your spawn point. It's a good idea to build your shelter close to the spawn point. This way you can easily reach it when you respawn.

Characters die frequently in Survival mode.

You don't want to be out in the open with only a shovel for protection when night falls.

You can build a shelter almost anywhere. It can be on a hilltop or a treetop, underground, in the sea, or even in the air! But one of the fastest and easiest ways to take cover is to burrow into a hillside. You can use your shovel and pickax to dig through the dirt and stone to create a small room for your first night. While you dig, you can collect the dirt and stones to save for later projects. You should also grab any nearby animals you come across, such as cows and pigs, for food.

It's best to use a shovel to dig a shelter in dirt, but you can do it with your bare hands if you have to.

Adding doors to your shelter can help make it feel like home.

Once you're finished digging, make sure to block the entrance to your hillside home by carving a wooden door. If you don't have much wood left, you can drop a dirt or stone block at the base of the entrance to act as a door. Then you'll be safe for the night.

CHAPTER 3
THE NIGHT SHIFT

IN *MINECRAFT*, NIGHTTIME LASTS SEVEN MINUTES. Later on in the game, you can create a bed that will allow you to sleep through the night. The bed also becomes your new spawn point. So each time you die, you will respawn in the last place you slept. But without a bed, you can spend the night crafting more items, cooking food, and digging deeper to mine materials.

A furnace is an essential part of every *Minecraft* shelter.

Along with a crafting table and tools, a furnace is important to have in *Minecraft*. You can use it to cook or to make materials such as metal or charcoal. With charcoal, you can make another important item: torches. They give you light and help you find your way. Since mobs spawn in dark places, torchlight will also keep mobs away. You can place torches all around your shelter. This will keep mobs away, and it will help you find your shelter the next time you leave.

STEMCRAFT

Heating an object causes a **chemical reaction** that changes the object and produces a new substance. In *Minecraft*, **smelting** a material in a furnace causes a chemical reaction. Smelting can melt, cook, or burn objects. It also can produce new materials. For example, wood becomes charcoal, sand becomes glass, and iron ore turns into iron ingots you can use to craft tools and armor.

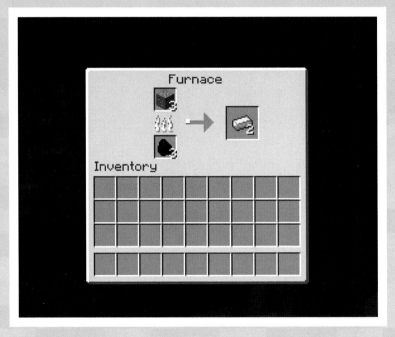

Using coal as fuel for your furnace is one way to turn iron ore into iron ingots.

One last important item to craft is a wooden chest. Typically, when you die in *Minecraft*, you drop all the tools you have crafted and the materials you have collected. When you respawn, you have to run around to collect all your items again. But if you keep your items in a chest, they will stay there. You won't lose anything if you die.

Make sure to store your valuable items in a chest before battling mobs.

As the game goes on, you can use your ten minutes of daylight more creatively. You can explore the world around you and dig mines to collect stone, iron, and even diamonds. With these ores, you can strengthen your tools and craft new ones, such as a hoe for farming and an ax to chop down trees. You can build bigger, better shelters. You can create a farm by planting **crops**

Players search for valuable materials by digging deep underground.

Building a farm means you'll always have a supply of food at home.

and keeping animals for food. You can get armor and new weapons to protect yourself and fight off hostile mobs. No matter what you do, the goal of Survival mode is always to do whatever it takes to stay alive.

CHAPTER 4

MORE
MINECRAFT

MINECRAFT IS A WORLD OF CREATIVITY, PROBLEM-SOLVING, AND SURVIVAL. In many ways, you are on your own as you figure out how to explore the world and what the best tools and **strategies** are.

DanTDM is one of *Minecraft*'s most famous gamers. His YouTube videos about the game have attracted millions of viewers.

The game also has a unique community of gamers who enjoy working together to make the game more challenging and more fun. These gamers post videos online to show how they play the game and help others learn new strategies. They create **tutorials** to teach new players how to get started and how to survive the first night in Survival mode. They also come up with challenges that other gamers can try out to improve their *Minecraft* skills.

CODECRAFT

Minecraft is a computer program. It processes one command after another. These commands are written in a special code computers understand, called Java. People who write computer code are programmers.

Writing computer code requires problem-solving. Sometimes programmers have to write lines of code many times before a program works. They look through lines of letters, numbers, and symbols to find the problem. Then they come up with a way to solve it.

Minecraft is also about problem-solving. The game doesn't give you instructions to tell you how to survive. Instead, you spawn into a world and have to figure out how to find resources, make tools, and build a shelter. You may die and respawn many times before figuring out how to survive the night.

Programming a video game takes a lot of practice.

Along with these videos and tutorials, *Minecraft* hosts
a number of community events where gamers can come
together to meet and share their ideas. At MineVention,
Minefaire, Blockfest, and MineCon, gamers can learn
more about *Minecraft*, participate in tournaments,
and meet other gamers and people who have created
popular tutorials and videos.

Minecraft's lead creative designer, Jens Bergensten (*left*), chats with
actor Will Arnett at MineCon in 2017.

Minecraft also frequently releases new versions and updates to the game. Sometimes this changes what it takes to survive or adds new elements or challenges. Update Aquatic was introduced in 2018. This version of the game includes new mobs and a new weapon. It's easier to build a shelter beneath the sea, and dolphins guide players and help them find

Update Aquatic opened a whole new world for *Minecraft* fans to explore.

Gamers are finding new ways to survive—and die—with Update Aquatic.

treasure. In *Minecraft* there is always somewhere new to explore, something new to create, or a new problem to solve. The game is sure to remain popular and exciting for years to come.

GLOSSARY

chemical reaction: a change that happens when two or more substances combine to form a new substance

crops: plants grown by farmers

hostile mobs: monsters in *Minecraft*

hotbar: the bottom row of inventory that can be accessed while you're playing *Minecraft*

inventory: a storage area for the items you collect as you play

ore: a block of material that is mined and collected in *Minecraft*

smelting: a method in *Minecraft* for obtaining resources by cooking, melting, or burning a substance

spawning: appearing in a new world for the first time

strategies: carefully developed plans for reaching a goal

tutorials: books, videos, or programs that teach someone how to do something

FURTHER INFORMATION

Miller, John. *Unofficial Minecraft STEM Lab for Kids: Family-Friendly Projects for Exploring Concepts in Science, Technology, Engineering, and Math*. Beverly, MA: Quarry Books, 2018.

Milton, Stephanie. *Minecraft: Guide to Exploration*. New York: Del Rey, 2017.

Milton, Stephanie. *Minecraft Essential Handbook*. New York: Scholastic, 2015.

Minecraft
https://minecraft.net/en-us/

Minecraft Wiki: Survival (Game Mode)
http://minecraft.wikia.com/wiki/Survival_(Game_mode)

Schwartz, Heather E. *The World of* Minecraft. Minneapolis: Lerner Publications, 2018.

Survival
https://minecraft.gamepedia.com/Survival

Surviving Your First Night in Survival Mode
https://www.howtogeek.com/school/htg-guide-to-minecraft/lesson7/

INDEX

PHOTO ACKNOWLEDGMENTS

Image credits: Various screenshots by Linda Zajac and Julia Zajac; DanTDM, *WHAT'S WRONG WITH THIS MINECRAFT HORSE?!?! [#2]* via YouTube, p. 25; Hero Images/Getty Images, p. 26; Minecraft, *MINECON Earth 2017 Livestream* via YouTube, p. 27; Design element: COLCU/Shutterstock.com.